Men Who Won the West

(Abridged from Famous Pioneers)

By FRANKLIN FOLSOM

Illustrated by DICK PRIEST

SCHOLASTIC BOOK SERVICES

NEW YORK · TORONTO · LONDON · AUCKLAND · SYDNEY

Contents

Copyright © 1955 by Sam'l Gabriel Sons & Co. Copyright © 1962 by Franklin Folsom. This edition is published by Scholastic Book Services, a division of Scholastic Magazines, Inc., by arrangement with the author and the Evelyn L. Singer Agency.

4th printing   January 1970   Printed in the U.S.A.

The Pioneer Spirit

One day out in Nebraska a stranger met a pioneer named Jack who was standing by his covered wagon.

"Where's your home?" the stranger asked.

"Hain't got no home," Jack replied.

"Where do you live then?"

"Where do I live!" Jack said scornfully. "Where do I live? I don't live nowhere. I'm marching ahead of civilization."

"Well, where do you sleep?"

"Sleep? I sleep where I like on the prairie, drink out of the North Platte, eat jack rabbits and raw wolf. But it's gettin' too crowded for me, stranger. I heard a whole family is comin' up the river to settle about fifty miles below here. So I'm leaving for the West tomorrow."

In the old days, pioneers were always leaving for the West, and the West kept going west until it couldn't go any farther. That was the pioneer spirit.

Daniel Boone

Indians!" Daniel Boone whispered to his friend John Stuart. "They've ketched us, John."

Boone and Stuart had been hunting and trapping in the Kentucky wilderness for seven months. In all that time they had not seen one Indian. But now they had run into trouble. They were surrounded.

" 'Twas my own fault," Boone said to himself. He'd been careless — but also unlucky. The white men and the Indians had been coming up opposite sides of a little hill and surprised each other at the top.

The Shawnees looked in silence at the white men's dirty buckskin clothes. One look was enough. Those splotches and smears came from grease and blood. Plainly Boone and Stuart had been killing and skinning deer — lots of deer. And they had been doing it in the Indians' own private hunting grounds.

"Show us your camp!" the Shawnee leader ordered. He spoke English, and white men had named him Captain Will.

Somewhere in the woods were five other men who had been helping Boone and Stuart with their hunting. Where were they now? Could they come to the rescue?

Boone was a superb woodsman, and he could travel as silently as any Indian. But from now on he pretended to be very clumsy. He broke twigs, stumbled, and made a general racket in the still forest. It was a trick to warn his five helpers.

Just as he hoped, Boone's noise alerted his men. But they did nothing to save the six horses at the camp, or the hides and furs that Boone had been collecting. The men simply ran away and hid.

Boone watched the Shawnees seize his traps, his fine muzzle-loading rifles, his gunsmithing tools, his horses. Then the Indians loaded the horses with several hundred buckskins, which were worth a dollar each, and dozens of beaver pelts worth a buckskin each — or as people said then and still say now, "a buck" apiece.

"These are ours," Captain Will said sternly. "They came from our hunting grounds. Now brothers, go home and stay there."

He handed Boone and Stuart a gun, moccasins to wear, a doeskin for patching them, and powder and shot enough so they could hunt for food on the long way to their homes in North Carolina. Boone and Stuart set out toward North Carolina along a well-marked trail known as the Warrior's Path. But they did not go far.

That night they turned back. Stealthily they crept up to
the Shawnees' camp. They located four of the six horses and
led them away. Then off they rode down the Warrior's Path
toward safety — they hoped.

At dawn the two white men stopped. Daniel Boone flung himself on the soft grass to rest. Stuart squatted down to fix a moccasin.

"What's that?" Boone asked suddenly.

A little noise had made him look up, and he found himself staring — at Captain Will! Behind the chief came a galloping band of Shawnees. And every one of them was laughing. The idea that two white men could expect to run off horses under their very noses!

Captain Will tied a horse bell around Boone's neck. Then he said, "Dance, brother!"

Boone decided he'd better dance, and he did, while the Indians laughed even harder. Still, they made no move to harm their captives. Instead, they promised to let the white men go free again — in a few days. First they wanted to get the horses safely across the Ohio River.

"Very well," said Daniel Boone. But he didn't care to wait that long. Slyly he and Stuart escaped one night. And this time they took good care not to be recaptured. Nevertheless, Daniel didn't give up and go back to North Carolina. His brother, Squire Boone, arrived shortly with fresh supplies, and Daniel stayed in the wilderness two more years. Then he went home to his beloved wife and children.

He was happier than ever before in his life. He and his brother Squire had been successful. Two valuable shipments of hides and furs had already gone out safely over the trail. The money they brought helped to support Daniel's family and to pay his debts. Now he had a third big batch to sell. And he had found new country where he wanted to settle down and live.

Before the Boones moved westward, Daniel helped to arrange a treaty with the Indians which allowed white men to settle in Indian hunting grounds. Then he led a whole group of families across the mountains to the land he loved. Starting along the Warriors' Path, they carved a road for their wagons through the forests and called it the Wilderness Road.

Kidnaped

Jemimah Boone, Daniel's daughter, felt quite safe in the new little village of Boonesborough which grew up on the bank of the Kentucky River. By the time she was fourteen, trouble with the Indians had died down. Her only worry

one Sunday afternoon was a cut in her foot that she'd got from walking around without any shoes.

"Let's go for a canoe ride," Jemimah said to her friends Betsy and Fanny Calloway. "My foot hurts, and I want to soak it in the water."

Betsy and Fanny paddled, while Jemimah steered and hung her sore foot over the side in the cool water. A little way below the village the canoe stuck on a sand bar.

Suddenly five Indians appeared from the brush and surrounded the girls. The girls screamed and whanged the men over the head with their paddles. But the Indians only laughed and took them captive.

Jemimah recognized the leader of the party. He was Chief Stomach-Hangs-Down, a Cherokee who had visited her father's cabin back in North Carolina. The chief disapproved of the treaty which gave Kentucky hunting grounds to white men. Now he had joined some Shawnee warriors, spying on Boonesborough and planning for an attack later on.

"I shan't go one step with you," Jemimah told the chief. "Do you know who I am? I am Wide-Mouth's daughter." That was the name the Cherokees had given Daniel Boone.

"Are these your sisters?" the chief asked in perfect English.

Jemimah thought fast. "Yes," she answered. It might help if the Indians thought all three girls were daughters of the famous frontiersman.

Chief Stomach-Hangs-Down smiled cheerfully. For once an Indian was going to get the better of Daniel Boone! No harm would come to the girls. They would be adopted by the Shawnees. They might feel homesick, but nothing worse would happen to them.

Of course Jemimah didn't want to be adopted, and as soon as the Indians were on the trail with their captives she thought of a scheme.

She felt sure that by now people at home would have missed her. A rescue party would be out searching. Hoping that they would hear, she cried: "Oh, my foot, my foot!"

The Indians paid no attention.

"My foot hurts!" Jemimah yelled as loud as she could, and she began to limp, walking as slowly as she could.

The chief gave her some moccasins. He also noticed that the girls' ankle-length dresses caught on briars. So he cut the skirts to half length and told the girls to wrap the cloth around their legs to protect them from scratches.

Gleefully, Jemimah, Fanny, and Betsy obeyed. This would give them just what they needed. They could leave threads and bits of torn cloth along their trail so that rescuers could follow them. But a whole day went by and no rescuers appeared. The girls pretended to be more and more tired. They hung onto bushes and broke off branches to leave more "sign" for pursuers to follow.

The Indians thought they were in luck when they found a stray horse. Jemimah, whose foot really did bother her, could ride now, and the party could move faster. But Jemimah had learned a trick or two from her father. She managed to go slower than ever by pretending she couldn't ride. Again and again she fell off. The Indians took time out to give all three girls riding lessons. Fanny tumbled off immediately. Betsy did a little better at first; then she too kept falling off, even after the exasperated horse whirled around and bit her!

The Indians were patient. They felt sure they had avoided pursuit by walking downstream and following along rocky ridges where no footprints showed. By the middle of the third day, Jemimah had lost all hope of rescue. The Indians killed a buffalo, built a small fire, and began to prepare their first cooked meal.

Daniel Boone had been taking his Sunday-afternoon nap when news came that his daughter Jemimah and her two friends must have been taken captive. Barefoot, and wearing his Sunday pants made of cloth, he grabbed his rifle and set off on the search. Many other men from the village went with him. At last they discovered the "sign" left by the girls. But it was almost dark by this time. During the night someone raced home for Daniel's moccasins and his buckskin clothes that wouldn't get torn by briars. At dawn they were following the "sign" again.

By noon of the third day Boone discovered a buffalo that had just been killed. He knew that he was close. The Indians would be cooking the meat beside the next stream.

Now he had to be very careful, for the Shawnees would kill the girls rather than give them up.

Noiselessly, Daniel and his men crept close, fired on the unsuspecting Indians, and drove them wounded into the brush. Chief Stomach-Hangs-Down would have been surprised to see how briskly the three girls walked home. Even Jemimah's sore foot no longer bothered her! For all of the Indians' craft in the woods, Daniel Boone and his quick-witted daughter had proved too courageous and too clever for them.

Daniel couldn't understand why the Shawnees had been hiding so close to Boonesborough that Sunday afternoon in July, 1776. But he soon found out. There was war between England and the Colonies. The British in Canada were now paying Indians to attack American settlements on the frontier. Although they didn't know it yet, the Declaration of Independence had been signed only three days before Jemimah was kidnaped.

Daniel Boone and Chief Blackfish

The housewives in Boonesborough needed salt. Daniel had to get it, even though the trip would be dangerous now that the British were paying the Indians to make raids on the white men. Besides, it was midwinter. Footprints would show plainly in the snow, and Indians could see them. Nevertheless, Daniel led thirty men to a salt spring he knew about. There they camped and boiled the water down in kettles to get the salt.

One day Boone left the others at work while he hunted alone for fresh meat. Suddenly a party of Shawnee warriors surrounded him. They took him unharmed to their camp. There he discovered a hundred fully armed warriors, plus a number of white men sent by the British.

This could only mean that an attack on Boonesborough was planned. What could Daniel do? While he was thinking, the Shawnees crowded around him. He was such a prize captive that they all wanted to shake his hand!

"Howdy," Boone said to their chief, Blackfish.

"Howdy," Blackfish answered gravely. "My scouts have seen your men making salt."

Now Daniel had even more to think about. This big party of warriors would capture or kill the saltmakers. Then they would fall upon Boonesborough. The British had offered a reward for any pioneer captives — or their scalps.

"I will arrange for my men to surrender, if you promise not to harm them," Boone said to Blackfish.

Blackfish agreed, and Daniel was sure he would keep his word.

Now Daniel said craftily, "You will have many captives. It will be hard to take women and children with you in this cold weather. I advise you to wait and capture Boonesborough in the spring."

Blackfish nodded. "I will leave the women and children till spring," he said. "But if the saltmakers do not surrender peacefully, you will be killed."

Boone went back and talked to his friends at the salt spring. They agreed there was nothing they could do but surrender. Through the snow they all marched off, prisoners of war, toward the British headquarters at Detroit.

Chief Blackfish took a great liking to Daniel Boone. He admired him so much that he refused to sell him to the British at Detroit, even though they offered a high price. Instead, he adopted Boone as his own son and showed him many kindnesses.

Boone pretended to become a good Shawnee. He allowed his long hair to be plucked out, Shawnee fashion, leaving only a scalp lock. Although he didn't particularly like this, there were many other things about Shawnee life that he liked and enjoyed. But when he saw his "father," Blackfish, preparing for a big raid on Boonesborough, he knew the time had come to escape. He must keep the Indians from suspecting his plan, and he did so in a very clever way.

When a group of hunters wasn't looking, Boone slipped the lead balls out of their muzzle-loading guns, but left the powder in. He hid the bullets in a piece of buckskin under his shirt.

"Brothers, I am going home," he called to them suddenly. And he started off.

"You are not going!" Blackfish commanded. "If you try, I will shoot you."

Boone kept on walking.

True to his word, Blackfish picked up his gun. So did the others. As they fired, Boone held the piece of buckskin in the air and pretended to be catching the bullets. After the smoke cleared away, there stood Daniel unharmed. In his hand were the lead balls he had "caught"— the same ones he had taken out of the Indians' guns a few minutes before.

"Here are your bullets," he said to the astonished Blackfish. "Boone ain't going away."

The trick worked like magic — which is what the Shawnees thought it was. They grew careless and didn't watch Daniel as closely as they had before.

One day he saw his chance when all the men were out hunting turkeys. Only the Indian women remained in their camp. Boldly he seized a horse, said "good-by" to his Shawnee "mother," and dashed for home.

Boone rode until his horse was nearly dead. Then he ran and walked the rest of the way. In four days he covered one hundred and sixty miles.

The warning Daniel brought saved Boonesborough. The people there had time enough to prepare for the attack. Although they were outnumbered seven to one, they managed to fight off the war party of Indians led by Canadian officers.

When the British lost the Revolutionary War, Indian attacks on the settlements died down. Before long, Boone left Kentucky and followed the frontier west to the banks of the Missouri River, where he lived in peace until he was almost eighty-six years old.

Lewis and Clark

Plans for a great secret expedition were underway. Thomas Jefferson, President of the United States, drew the plans up himself. Then, to carry them out, he picked the young man he trusted most in the whole country: tall, bowlegged Captain Meriwether Lewis.

The dangers of the expedition were so great that two commanders were needed in case something should happen to one of them. So Captain Lewis wrote to his redheaded friend, William Clark. "Will you go?" he asked Clark.

Together the two men would explore the whole new territory which the United States had just bought from France. It stretched from the Mississippi River to the Rocky

Mountains, and no American explorers had yet gone over-land across it and on to the Pacific Ocean. Along the way they would have to pass through the territory of dozens of Indian tribes who might be hostile.

But why was the secrecy necessary? England and Spain also had their eyes on the West. They might stir up all kinds of trouble for rival explorers from the United States.

Clark wrote back to Lewis:

> *"This is an amence undertaking fraited with numerous dificulties, but my freind I Join with you my hand & Heart."*

Clark couldn't spell, but both he and Lewis were skilled frontiersmen and remarkable leaders of men. If anybody could find out all about the new land that President Jefferson had bought, they could.

Even the Army, which prepared all the equipment for Lewis and Clark, was not told where they were going. When the flatboat and the canoes carrying their supplies moved up the Missouri River past Daniel Boone's new home, neither Boone nor anyone else suspected what was going on. Lewis and Clark might have been ordinary traders. A great Newfoundland dog barked from the deck of their boat. One man had a fiddle which he played every night while the rest of the crew danced. These things, together with a remarkable newfangled air rifle which Lewis had, all proved in the end to be of real importance to the success of an amazing adventure.

Lewis and Clark set out from St. Louis, Missouri—May, 1804. All summer and late into fall the men paddled and

pushed and pulled the boats against the current of the Missouri River. Then they built log cabins and settled for the winter near a Mandan Indian village in North Dakota.

All winter long the white men told the Mandan Indians tall tales. One of them was about a great animal back east.

"It has no mouth," they said. "It gets food only through its nose, by breathing in the steam from cooking meat."

The Mandans told stories, too. They spoke of an animal so huge and fierce that it took ten warriors with bows and arrows to kill one. After it had been skinned, two men could scarcely carry its hide. The white men, they said, would certainly meet these animals when they started up the river in the spring.

Of course, nobody believed the Mandans' stories. After all, Lewis was a scientist. He had never seen or even read about a beast like this. But after the boats had traveled a little way farther upriver, Lewis quickly changed his mind.

Six of his men went ashore one day and crept up on a sleeping animal. Four of them confidently fired and hit it. Up rose a bear — a grizzly bear — and he was merely angered by the four bullets. The grizzly charged. Two more shots hit him, and still he didn't stop. The men ran

all in a bunch to the river, then scattered. The bear paused,
undecided which ones to follow. This gave the hunters
a chance to reload. Some of them fired again. Furiously the
bear charged them. Two men leaped over the twenty-foot
bank into the river. The grizzly followed, almost on top
of them.

Only when the bear was slowed by the current did a
man on shore stop him with a bullet through his brain. That
was the only way to kill a grizzly with a low-powered
muzzle-loading gun.

Day after day men had narrow escapes from bears. Even
at night they wouldn't have been safe if it hadn't been for
Scammon, the enormous Newfoundland dog. When grizzlies
tried to enter the camp, Scammon frightened them off with
barks that were as big as he was.

Important People

"Make friends with the Indians," President Jefferson had said to Captain Lewis. So Lewis took along great bales of presents for the Indians, to show that he wanted peace with them.

But some things he hadn't counted on turned out to be equally important. One was the fiddle that Private Peter Cruzat played. Another was the square dancing that the other men did to his music.

Almost every night the members of the expedition danced. Half of them wore white armbands to show that they were "ladies" in the squares. Indians, who loved dancing themselves, were fascinated by the white men's performances.

After the dancing, Lewis sometimes showed off his marvelous air rifle. He had brought it along for emergencies —in case he ran out of powder. It worked very much like our popguns. The Indians were delighted with its "magic" power.

One person on the expedition was particularly important. This was a Shoshone Indian girl called Sacajawea, or Bird-Woman. Lewis and Clark had hired Bird-Woman's French-Canadian husband to be their guide. In the end, she and her baby were ten times more valuable than he. The sight of a woman and a baby convinced Indians along the way that this was no war party.

Smoke Signals

"Look there — a smoke signal!" Clark exclaimed one day.

"I can't understand it," Lewis replied. "The signals mean that the Shoshones know we are here. But why are they hiding?"

Clark shook his head. For more than two thousand miles Indians had swarmed down to the riverbanks to see these strange men who had beards on their faces. Now the one tribe they simply had to find was avoiding them. The success of the whole expedition depended on meeting the Shoshones and getting horses from them.

Lewis sighed wearily. He thought again about the two thousand miles they had come. Every inch of the way had been a struggle upstream against the treacherous Missouri River. The last eighteen miles were the worst. Here they had been forced to carry their boats and supplies overland around the falls of the Missouri. It had taken his entire crew more than a month of heroic labor to travel just eighteen miles! And now failure lay ahead unless they could get horses.

High mountains rose in the distance. The explorers would have to abandon their boats, and the men could not carry everything on their backs. Bird-Woman had told them that her people would sell them horses. But you couldn't get horses from people until you could meet and talk to them.

"We have no time to lose," Lewis said. "Winter will catch us in the mountains. I must go ahead of the boats."

Clark wished he could go instead. But he had a badly infected ankle. Therefore, Lewis with his three companions, hiked ahead over the cactus-covered flatland, following first one trail and then another. There was plenty of Indian "sign," but no sign of an Indian.

Lewis sent one of his men scouting far to the right and the other far to the left. He and the third man walked straight ahead. Every few yards he paused to look through

his telescope. Suddenly the figure of a mounted Indian filled the lens.

"At last!" Lewis cried in great excitement. "Can you see him? A horseman!"

Soon the horseman saw Lewis and stopped.

Above all, Lewis wanted not to frighten him away. Bird-Woman had told him what to do. Quickly he slipped his pack off his back and got out a blanket. He waved it above his head and then laid it on the ground. In Indian sign language, this meant "Friendship." Lewis repeated the sign three times.

The Indian saw the signal. But he also saw Lewis' scouts who kept advancing. This looked suspiciously like a trap. The two might close in on him from behind, while he went toward the man with the blanket.

The two scouts were so absorbed that they did not look back at Lewis for a prearranged signal to stop. In desperation, Lewis shouted, "Tab-ba-bone!"

The Shoshone began to back up.

"Tab-ba-bone!" Lewis cried again, moving forward.

The Shoshone hesitated a moment longer, then suddenly wheeled his horse and galloped off. Only later did Lewis discover what his mistake had been. He thought he was shouting the Shoshone word for "white man." But he had mispronounced it. What he actually said was a word that meant "stranger" or "enemy"!

No wonder the Shoshone was suspicious. Here was a man who signaled "friendship" and then cried "enemy," while two others seemed ready to pounce from either side.

Lewis was in despair. The Shoshone would probably warn his people to run away. That would mean no horses, and an end to the expedition. Or the Shoshone might come back with warriors. And that would mean the end of Lewis!

To prove he was friendly, Lewis built a large fire on a hilltop. No enemy of the Shoshones would advertise himself so plainly. He left gifts by the fire, then moved on.

Next day he came upon two women and a man. They, too, fled when he called "Tab-ba-bone!" Soon he found a well-marked trail, and beside it two women and a girl.

Immediately Lewis offered them presents of beads and a mirror. Then he pulled out some vermillion paint and smeared it on their faces. Bird-Woman had told him that this color meant "Peace" among the Shoshones. Meantime, one of Lewis' scouts, who knew sign language, was explaining as fast as he could.

"Friendly white men want to go to the Shoshone village."

The women led the way. But word had already reached the village that strangers had captured the women. A Shoshone war party came dashing to the rescue.

Lewis stood face to face with sixty angry warriors, armed with bows and arrows. Unless he did the right thing, this would be the end.

Quickly Lewis dropped his gun. He walked boldly toward the warriors, holding only the American flag. Then the women came to his rescue. Gleefully they showed the presents he'd given them. Lewis and his men were not enemies.

"Ah-hi-e! Ah-hi-e!" the Shoshones began to exclaim, meaning, "Glad to meet you."

One by one the warriors embraced the white men. Then there was more Shoshone etiquette that had to be observed. Lewis lit the peace pipe he had brought and passed it around. Finally everyone went to the village. Here Lewis had to sit down and take off his moccasins while he talked to the chief. This was a Shoshone way of promising to tell the truth. It meant, "May I walk barefoot the rest of my life if I tell a lie." This was no country in which to go barefoot. Sharp rocks and cactus plants were everywhere.

Lewis invited the Shoshones to go back to the river with him.

Meantime, Clark was worrying. What had happened to Lewis and the scouts?

Clark and Bird-Woman set out to look for them. All of a sudden Clark paused in complete astonishment. Bird-Woman, walking ahead of him, broke into a dance. Then she signaled excitedly in sign language, sucking on her fingers. The sign meant, "People among whom I was suckled." She had seen the Shoshones coming with Lewis toward the river.

In even greater astonishment Clark watched what happened next. A Shoshone girl rushed toward Bird-Woman and embraced her. They were old friends. Lewis had stumbled upon Bird-Woman's own particular band of Shoshones.

When Lewis and Clark sat down with the chief to begin the ceremony of bargaining for horses, they asked Bird-Woman to interpret for them. More excitement — the chief was Bird-Woman's brother! He hadn't seen her since the day, five years before, when she had been kidnaped by an enemy tribe.

Bird-Woman, who liked the whites, helped them buy horses from her people. Now the Lewis and Clark expedition could go on. It could go beyond the land that President Jefferson had bought from France.

Bird-Woman accompanied the explorers across the mountains. When they ran out of food, she taught them to feed themselves on roots and berries, and the hidden foodstores of little animals in country where there was no big game. Finally they reached the Pacific coast, in November, 1805. The secret trip from St. Louis had taken a year and a half. The overland route to the Northwest had been opened.

John Colter

I'm not going back," John Colter told Lewis and Clark one day when the exploring party was on the way home. Colter had fallen in love with the wilderness, and now he'd made up his mind not to leave it. So Lewis and Clark gave him permission to stay behind.

It was a dangerous life Colter had decided on, but he was full of confidence. He'd learned from Lewis and Clark how to get along with the Indians. And he was offered a job by a trader named Manuel Lisa who had a lonely little fort on the Big Horn River. Lisa did business with fur trappers and with Indians. He felt sure that a man who had Colter's experience would be just what he needed.

"I want you to go and make a deal with the Blackfeet," Lisa said. "They don't allow white men to trap in their hunting grounds, but I think you can arrange for me to trade with them."

"When do I start?" Colter replied. Nothing could have suited him better.

"On the way, you can visit the Crows and bargain with them too," Lisa went on.

Full of enthusiasm, Colter set out. Up to now the Blackfeet had always traded with the Canadians. Perhaps he could win them over to trading with Lisa instead.

The scheme appeared harmless enough. John Colter had no way of knowing what terrible trouble it would bring to all the white men who came along later.

Traveling on foot, Colter hurried across the five hundred miles to Crow country. The Crows agreed to let Lisa come and trade. Then, reluctantly, they said they would guide Colter into Blackfoot country farther west.

Before long he found out why the Crows had hesitated, and why he should never have asked them to go. Blackfoot warriors ambushed the Crows, who were their ancient enemies. Colter tried to stay out of the fight, but he couldn't. In the end he killed a Blackfoot and was wounded himself. Now he could never expect to go among the Blackfeet as a friend.

When his wound healed, Colter headed back for Lisa's fort, taking a short cut through new country. And one day he came upon a sight that amazed and thrilled him.

Great fountains of water shot up out of the earth. Caverns in the rocks rumbled. The air smelled of sulphur. In one place Colter saw a pool of boiling mud; in another, springs hot enough to cook meat.

Later, when he told people what he had seen, they smiled and tapped their heads and spoke of "Colter's Hell."

It was many years before anyone believed that he wasn't either lying or a bit crazy.

The place Colter had discovered was, of course, Yellowstone Park.

Blackfeet Become Enemies

"Go back to Blackfoot country in the spring," Lisa ordered Colter. "There's not one chance in a thousand that you'll meet a Blackfoot who recognizes you. I still think you can make a deal with them."

Colter wasn't so sure, but he set out anyway with another man named Potts. One morning they were paddling their canoe along a river when hundreds of Blackfeet appeared on each bank.

"Come ashore!" the Indians signaled in sign language. At least they did not greet the white men with a shower of arrows. Still, Colter knew he had to make friends with the Blackfeet right now.

"Be careful," he said to Potts. "We must make no quick moves."

But Potts was so terrified that he forgot. When the two men beached their canoe, the Blackfeet asked Potts for his gun. Instead of handing it over boldly, Potts jumped into the canoe and shoved off.

To the Blackfeet, this meant just one thing: the man was both a coward and an enemy. A moment later, he proved it. In a panic, he fired his gun, killing a Blackfoot. A cloud of arrows descended on him, and he was dead. From this day on it would be war to the finish between white men and Blackfeet.

Luckily for Colter, the Blackfoot warrior always gave strong, brave prisoners a chance to survive. The captive, naked, was allowed a long headstart in a race for his life. Warriors followed him. It was then a test of speed and endurance.

"Can you run?" the chief asked at last.

"I'm no good," Colter said, hoping to make the Blackfeet think they would have no trouble catching him. Actually, he was a wonderful runner.

The trick worked.

The Blackfeet took all his clothes — even his moccasins. Then they sent him three hundred yards off on the cactus-covered plain.

"Run!" the chief cried, and at the same time he signaled his warriors.

Colter ran like the wind. And he kept on running, in spite of the cactus spines that stabbed his bare feet. After

three miles, he had left all but one of the warriors far behind. That one was gaining on him.

Suddenly, Colter stopped and turned. The Blackfoot was so surprised that his own weary legs betrayed him. He stumbled and fell. Colter was on him in a flash, and the lance intended for the white man went into the warrior instead.

A river lay ahead. Colter dived in and hid beneath a pile of driftwood. There he stayed all day long under water, getting air through a hollow reed he held in his mouth.

Finally the Blackfeet gave up the search, and seven days afterward Colter struggled into Lisa's fort.

Later he and others did a great deal of beaver trapping in the western wilderness. But only the bravest — or the most foolish — sought to take beaver from Blackfoot streams.

Zebulon M. Pike

Young Lieutenant Pike felt cheerful. He had returned safely from a long, dangerous exploring trip up the Mississippi River. Less than two weeks ago, he'd led his men back into Army headquarters near the frontier town of St. Louis. Now General Wilkinson wanted to talk with him about a new assignment. Pike hoped he would be sent back East. He knew he wasn't a born explorer, like Lewis or Clark.

"These are your orders," General Wilkinson said, handing Pike an envelope. Then he went on, "But I have other orders for you which cannot be written down."

The young lieutenant listened with growing amazement. He, Zebulon M. Pike, was being asked to be a spy as well as an explorer!

The written orders were plain and simple: Pike was to go west through territory that the United States had recently bought from France. He was to make peace among the Indians of the plains. He was to explore the headwaters of the Arkansas River, and find the headwaters of the Red River. Then he was to follow the Red River down to the place where it joined the Mississippi.

This part of the country was vast and unmapped. Nobody knew for sure which part of it belonged to the United States and which part belonged to Spain. Both countries wanted to claim as much of it as possible.

Spanish pioneers had been moving northward from Mexico, just as pioneers from the United States had been moving westward. Some of the Spaniards had settled in California, far away on the Pacific Coast. But right now General Wilkinson wasn't thinking about them. He was interested in the Spanish-held area we now call New Mexico and Texas.

"Find out all you can about the Spaniards and their plans," Wilkinson said.

"But, sir, I can't speak Spanish," Pike answered.

"I know that. But you speak French. You will find interpreters who know French, even if they don't know English."

"Very well, sir," Pike said.

"Perhaps the best plan would be to get yourself captured," Wilkinson went on. "If soldiers capture you, they will take you to a high officer in the Spanish army. As a prisoner, you will get a chance to travel in Mexico."

Pike looked a little doubtful.

"Naturally, the Spaniards will have to set you free before too long," the general went on. "You will be carrying these orders which tell you *not* to go into Spanish territory, but you cannot be blamed if you happen to lose your way in the wilderness. Good luck!"

Zebulon Pike didn't like pioneering, but he carried out orders — no matter how dangerous they were.

So, in July, 1806, he headed for the West. In his party were a doctor and less than two dozen soldiers, who knew only that they were supposed to explore the Arkansas and the Red rivers. Just before they left, Pike remembered to slip a certain book into his pack — a French grammar which he could study to refresh his knowledge of the language.

The trip was hard, but not very unusual. The men pushed and pulled a keelboat up the Missouri River, then up the Osage River. From there they traveled over strange prairie country on horseback to the Arkansas River. On the way they met Indian tribes, and Pike persuaded them to stop fighting each other. All this was just what his written orders called for.

But so far Pike had failed to get himself captured by the Spaniards! He hadn't seen even one Spanish soldier, although he had followed the trail left by about three hundred of them who had gone far up into Kansas. The Spanish trail led into the mountains, so into the mountains went Pike, right past the tremendous peak that we now call Pikes Peak. Snow covered the trail, and Pike had to find his way as best he could.

Soon the thermometer showed twelve degrees below zero. Pike's men wore moccasins, but they had no socks! Near the middle of January, nine of them had feet so badly frozen they couldn't travel. And there had been nothing to eat for two days.

Now the commander of the expedition had to become a hunter in order to feed his men. In deep snow, Pike set out with three others. A whole day went by, and they saw only one animal — a buffalo. Their shots failed to bring down the huge beast. Pike didn't know that a bullet from his low-powered gun had to hit a certain spot right behind a buffalo's shoulder in order to kill it. He wasn't a very good shot anyway. But he was determined.

"We can't go back without meat," he said. "The disappointment would be more than the others could bear." And so, nearly freezing, the four of them spent the night out on a snowy, rocky hillside.

"Buffalo!" Pike said to his numb companions the next morning. He had sighted a herd about a mile away.

They crawled painfully through the snow and got within range. But again their shots only sent the animals lumbering away. It was now four days since any of the men had eaten. They were almost too weak and cold to move. Even the stubborn, courageous Pike had given up all hope of living more than a few hours longer. And then he spied more buffalo.

With his last remaining strength, Pike managed to run a little way toward the herd without being seen. This time a lucky shot killed one beast. That night everyone had buffalo steak. Pike's expedition was saved.

With no map to follow, often without food, Pike and a few of his men struggled through deep snow, up over a high mountain range into a wide, beautiful valley with a river running through it.

"The Red River!" the men cried. All through these bitter weeks they had thought they were hunting for the source of the Red River. Now, they believed, their hardships had gotten them somewhere. But they were wrong: what they saw was the Rio Grande at a spot not far from a Spanish settlement.

Pike talked things over quietly with Dr. John Robinson, who had come along to serve as surgeon for the expedition and to help gather information about the Spaniards.

"Now it is up to you to make sure that the Spaniards find me," said Pike to the doctor. "You can go down to their settlements along this river. Say that you are on a business trip — you have to collect a debt for a friend — and that on the way you saw me. Meanwhile I'll build a fort to protect our party from Indians. When the Spaniards come, I'll be the most surprised man in the world to find that I'm on their territory. I'll be full of apologies."

While the doctor was gone, Pike had his men build a small log fort. It would give protection in case either the Indians or the Spaniards decided to fight. Around the fort ran a moat filled with water. The walls were strong enough to stand a heavy attack. In order to get in, a man had to crawl along a plank over the moat and through a small hole at the bottom of the log wall.

Now Pike was almost ready. He got out his French grammar, which he had carried all the way during the terrible struggle through snow and over the high mountain pass. Then he sat down to polish up his French while he waited to be captured.

Before long two men on horseback appeared. Pike did his best to act friendly. At last he was able to lure them up close. One of them turned out to be a Spanish soldier. The other was a Pueblo Indian. They were spies sent out to discover whether Dr. Robinson was telling the truth.

The two mysterious horse-men left. Now Pike decided he'd better post a guard to watch out for the troops he hoped would follow the spies. Meanwhile he kept studying his grammar book.

"Boom!" went the guard's gun one day — a signal that Spaniards had been seen. Soon two officers appeared. To Pike's delight, they spoke French. He hadn't been wasting his time! Behind the officers marched a hundred armed soldiers. They had come, they said, "to protect" the Americans from the Ute Indians.

Everything was very polite. Pike invited the two elegant Spanish officers into his fort. He kept a perfectly straight face while they got down and crawled along the plank and through the tiny opening into the fort.

"Will you have breakfast with me?" he asked the officers.
"Yes, thank you."

Pike gave them food he had got from their own Pueblo Indian spy a few days before — venison, goose, cornmeal mush, biscuits.

Of course, Pike pretended he was very much surprised when they told him that he was on the Rio Grande, not the Red River. The Spaniards pretended they wanted to be very helpful. They would protect him with a large force of soldiers who would guide him to the Red River.

From now on everything happened just as Pike had hoped. He was taken from settlement to settlement down the Rio Grande. He met the highest Spanish officials and learned a great deal about the country. Spain didn't want to make the United States angry, so Pike and his men were very well treated.

Finally Pike was allowed to go home — by way of the Red River! He had explored new country while he was a military prisoner, which is quite a trick.

Davy Crockett

Davy Crockett was the greatest bear hunter on the whole frontier. One year he and his dogs got seventeen bears the week before Christmas in the wildest part of west Tennessee. That was enough meat to last Davy and his family a long time, and he could sell the hides for a good price. Davy was all set to celebrate the holiday, shooting off gunpowder on Christmas Day, the way people did in those times.

But Davy and his little boy happened to stop in at the cabin of his friend McDaniel. Now McDaniel was a greenhorn, and Davy found he had no meat for Christmas.

"Come along," said Davy. "We'll just get you an eternal great fat bear."

Davy *hoped* they would. "It's turned mighty cold," he said to his little boy. "Maybe the bears have gone to house." Davy meant they might have crawled into warm holes to hibernate till spring.

Even when his dogs couldn't smell a bear, Davy was such a good hunter that he could find one anyway. He looked high in the trees. At last, in one big oak, he saw a hole. Below it were marks of bear claws.

"There's a bear in there," said Davy.

"How do you know?" McDaniel asked.

"He clumb the tree but he didn't come down."

"What makes you so sure?"

"When bears go up, they don't slip a bit. But when they come down, they make long scratches with their nails."

Just then the dogs began to bark, and away they went like a thundergust. Davy knew they had found a bear that hadn't hibernated yet. He and McDaniel rode off, killed the bear, then came back to the hollow tree where they'd left Davy's little boy. The boy was chopping away on the tree with his tomahawk.

But this bear didn't wait for the tree to fall before he woke up. The knocking roused him, and he poked his head out of the hole.

"Thar he comes!" Crockett hollered.

McDaniel caught up his gun and fired. As soon as the bear touched the ground, the dogs were all around it in a roll-and-tumble fight. Bear and dogs went down the hill in a squirming heap. Davy ran after them, and while the dogs were a-wooling away on it, he put his gun against the bear and killed it. Then he and his little boy and McDaniel went home for Christmas.

By spring Davy had killed a hundred and five bears.

That's a lot of bears for one man. People got to talking about Davy Crockett, and the more they talked the bigger the stories grew. Some folks said that he salted his bear steaks with hailstones, peppered them with buckshot, and fried them with streaks of lightning. They said he tamed a thirty-seven-foot alligator and used it for a bench in front of his cabin. They said he had such a powerful grin that he didn't need to shoot small game at all. He just grinned at possums and raccoons, and the critters would give up, then and there.

The real Davy Crockett was just as popular with his neighbors as the stories about him were. Many of his friends had seen him in action in the War of 1812, and they knew he was brave and quick and a good leader.

When the war broke out, the British persuaded a group of Creek Indians to attack an American settlement on the frontier and murder every man, woman, and child in it. Crockett knew this kind of thing had to be stopped. He joined the army under General Andrew Jackson.

Davy fought in one battle to defend two hundred friendly Creeks from an attack by eleven hundred Creeks who were on the British side. In another battle, he helped to save the American army from ambush. It happened this way:

Davy, with some other scouts, was riding along at the rear of the army. That was where General Jackson suspected trouble would come. Jackson was right. All of a sudden a thousand Indian warriors let loose against the American troops a volley "as hot as fresh mustard on a sore shin." Some of the soldiers and their officers fled.

Davy and his scouts had just started to ride across a

river. They turned their horses and charged straight into
the middle of the Creek warriors, who were confidently
giving their bloodcurdling yells. But Davy surprised and
confused them. They couldn't believe such a tiny band
would dare to attack. Davy galloped on and split the Creek
army in the middle. The two halves ran in opposite directions. With Davy and his scouts chasing them, the warriors

melted away among the hills. Crockett's handful of men had saved General Jackson's whole army.

At last, when the war was over, Jackson signed a peace treaty with the Indians. The treaty took away half of the Creeks' land, as punishment because they had helped the British. But Jackson promised the Indians they could live forever on the land that they were allowed to keep. Davy thought this was fair enough.

Later on General Jackson became President of the United States, and Davy's neighbors elected Davy to Congress. There had never been a hunter from the backwoods in Congress before.

Davy wasn't sure he'd like to live away from the wilderness. He didn't know how to read and write very well, but he figured he could learn — and he did, mighty fast.

At first people laughed at him and called him the "Coonskin Congressman." But Davy paid no attention. He was just as smart and just as fearless in Washington as he'd been in the wilderness. His motto was, "Be sure you're right. Then *go ahead.*"

Pretty soon Davy decided that President Jackson was wrong about something. The President wanted to break his treaty with the Indians. He said they had to move away from the land where he'd promised them they could live forever. Davy knew the Indians well. He had lived peacefully among them for years. So he got very angry about the broken promise. He said it wasn't fair to make them move away. In Congress and everywhere else he did his level best to help them keep their lands. But he lost the fight. And when the next election came up, all the politicians were against him, so he lost that, too.

Davy decided it was time for him to go on to a new frontier.

Davy Crockett started out for Texas, where there was a lot of new land to settle on. Besides, the Texans were fighting a war to get their independence from Mexico. The idea of independence appealed to Davy. So in the year 1836 he decided to join the fighting.

People in Texas had already heard of Davy Crockett. They fired cannon in his honor and asked him to a big celebration. Then and there he swore allegiance to the new, independent country of Texas.

"I will bear true allegiance to any future government that may hereafter be declared," the oath read.

"If you will add one word, I'll sign this," Davy said.

"What's that?"

"My oath must say 'future *republican* government,'" Davy answered. He was no man to support a king or a dictator. "We must govern ourselves as freemen should be governed."

"We're with you," the Texans said, and the word *republican* was added.

Jim Bridger

I'll bet you're wrong!"

"I'll bet I'm right!" Jim Bridger said.

Talk like this had been going on for days among the trappers. All of them were arguing about the Bear River, a most peculiar stream. It flowed north out of Bear Lake then made a hairpin turn and flowed back south. Where did it end? Did it turn north again and meet the Columbia River? Did it turn west to the Pacific Ocean?

"There's only one way to find out," twenty-year-old Jim Bridger announced. "This hoss is going down it and see."

That was the way Jim always did things. If there was something he didn't know, he went personally to find out.

For a trip down the Bear, he'd need a boat, and he set about building one. He had learned from Indians just what to do. First he cut green willow branches and stuck the large ends in a circle in the ground. Then he bent the branches in toward the center and wove them into a big basket.

Using rawhide thongs, he lashed the framework together. Next he stretched pieces of fresh buffalo hide over the basket with the hair side against the framework. He fitted and stitched the pieces of skin carefully together and coated the seams with buffalo tallow. Finally, he built a small smoky fire on the ground inside the whole thing. As the fresh skin dried out, it pulled tightly together around the frame. The tallow filled every crack.

After the hide was cured in this way, Jim had a bowl-shaped boat called a bullboat. He carved himself a paddle and was ready to take off.

The bullboat was small — just big enough to hold Jim's six-foot frame and his gun. He was an expert hunter, and he didn't have to take food along. He needed little but a gun, a knife, and extra moccasins. There was no telling how far he'd have to hike back.

"You git back before snow flies," one of the older men advised him. The leaves of the box elder, cottonwood and aspen were already turning gold and orange.

"Be careful of yore skulp," another warned. There might be hostile Indians along the way who would scalp Jim.

Jim grinned and waved good-by to the band of Mountain Men. In no time he was bobbing swiftly down the tumultuous Bear River. It was no easy trick to steer the round bullboat through the rapids and away from jutting boulders. Several hours of it were enough even for Jim's tough muscles. He was glad when the river passed out of a steep canyon and flowed more smoothly. Here he pulled the bullboat onto the shore and climbed to a high point for a look around.

Ahead of him the land flattened out. And far in the distance, perhaps twenty-five miles away, a huge body of water appeared. The sun glistened on its shining white shore.

Much sooner than he expected, Jim had seen where the Bear River ended!

Full of excitement, he ran back to his boat and paddled onward. The country grew more and more barren — almost like a desert. But at last Jim knew he'd reached the river mouth. And something strange was happening. His boat seemed to bob higher on the water. The whole place smelled peculiar, too.

More curious than ever, Jim scooped up some water in his hand. It tasted salty!

"By gawr!" Jim said aloud. "The Pacific."

Jim had settled the argument with his friends. He'd found the end of the Bear River. But it wasn't the Pacific Ocean he'd tasted. It was the Great Salt Lake of Utah.

Jim Bridger expected his friend Jedediah Smith to join the other Mountain Men in their camp any day now. He had known Jed ever since the two of them started out together for the Rocky Mountains when they were teen-agers.

No matter what happened, Jed always looked neater than most Mountain Men. He was shaved and he kept his long hair evenly trimmed. Nobody dared to joke about this. All the trappers had great respect for his courage and skill as a hunter. But they knew he had no sense of humor at all.

When Jed arrived, he brought news that sent Jim Bridger into a fever of excitement.

"I'm sure I found the strange place that Colter talked about," Jed said. "God has more wonders there than a man ever saw anywhere else on earth."

Jim knew that Jed was a deeply religious man. If he reported natural marvels, he must be telling the truth. Then and there, Jim Bridger decided to see this strange place for himself. And he did.

Jim was fascinated by the wonders he found. He tried to figure out what made the geysers spout. Why was a river icy cold in one spot and very warm farther downstream?

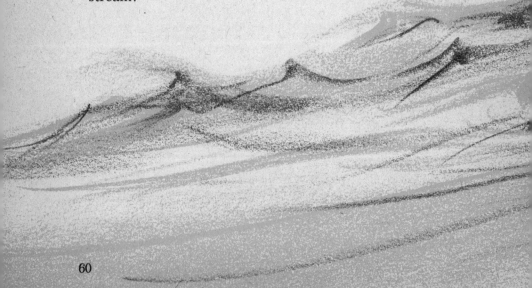

"I saw a mountain made entirely of black glass," Jim reported to his friends. "That's where the Indians get the stuff for those black obsidian arrowheads of theirs."

The other Mountain Men smiled. They thought Jim was telling tall tales. Before long, he heard one of them saying to a greenhorn:

"Bridger's seen some mighty strange things in these mountains. One day he came on a heap of birds, all of 'em lying with their heads bashed in. He started to ride on and his horse fell down. Knocked out. He'd run head on into a hill of pure glass. The birds couldn't see it. Neither could his horse. They tried to go through, and of course they knocked themselves out."

Jim let this one pass. But the next time a greenhorn happened along, he got in there first.

"I was hunting last fall," Bridger said solemnly, "and I sighted an elk drinking at a stream. I fired. He never so much as lifted his head at the sound. I fired again. Still he didn't budge. I decided to move in closer. Something stopped me. I found myself smack up against a mountain of glass. Magnifying glass, too. That elk I'd been shooting at was on the other side — fifteen miles away.

An Arrow in the Back

No one could doubt one thing that Jim Bridger discovered in the Yellowstone area — fine beaver pelts. The Yellowstone was country claimed by the proud Blackfeet who fought fiercely to keep their hunting grounds for themselves. But, danger or no danger, Jim determined to go back and get as many beaver as he could.

But soon Jim got himself into trouble. He and a party of other Mountain Men met a large Blackfoot band. The Indians made friendly signs and sent a small group of warriors out with a pipe of peace. Jim, with an equal number of Mountain Men, rode forward to meet the

Indians. The chief came on foot and unarmed, according to the custom of peace conferences. But Jim feared a trap. So he stayed on his horse and carried his gun. Worse than that, he cocked his gun, and the chief heard the telltale click.

Now it was the chief's turn to fear treachery. Instantly he grabbed Bridger's gun and pulled him from his horse. Blackfoot warriors, seeing the scuffle, came to their chief's rescue and sent two arrows into Jim's back. The chief leapt on Jim's horse and dashed out of range of the Mountain Men.

A day-long battle followed, with each side sniping at the other. There was no victory either way, but when the fighting was over, Bridger's men could get only one of the arrowheads out of his back.

The Blackfeet had made the arrowheads out of an old iron skillet. Jim wished they had used black glass instead, because one of the iron points bent and stuck like a fish-hook near his spine. There it stayed — a constant, painful reminder that Jim Bridger had made a mistake. He had rattled his gun at a peace conference. He couldn't blame the Indians for being suspicious. But he didn't leave the Yellowstone until he had a big pack of the very finest beaver pelts.

Joe Meek

With Jim Bridger, on one of his trips to the Yellowstone area, went a famous trapper named Joe Meek. Now "meek" was the one thing you couldn't call Joe, but one day he did have to act that way for a while. He was setting traps alone when a party of Crows captured him. Oddly enough, the chief of the Crows was named The Bold.

"All white men are liars," The Bold told Joe, who understood the Crow language. "But if you answer my questions truthfully I'll let you live."

"I'll tell you the truth," Joe promised. There was nothing else he could say if he wanted to keep his scalp. He would answer the questions as he thought best and then hope that luck was with him.

"Who is the leader of your party?" asked The Bold.

"Jim Bridger, the man you call Blanket Chief," Joe answered truthfully. Then he added something he hoped would put the Crows off guard. "Bridger has forty men."

The fact was that Bridger's party was six times that large, including friendly Indians with their families.

The Bold had enough warriors in his band to surprise and scalp forty men.

"Where is Blanket Chief's camp?" The Bold demanded.

Joe told the truth again. He had to let Bridger know that he was a captive, and he could do so only if the Crows took him up close to the Mountain Men's camp.

The Crows prepared for battle and started on Bridger's trail. Four days later they sighted Bridger's camp.

Swapping Prisoners

Now Joe's situation was desperate. The Bold took one look at Bridger's camp and saw that Joe had lied about the number of men there. Any minute the chief might carry out his promise and have Joe killed.

But Jim Bridger had guards of his own on duty. One of them discovered the Crows immediately and rode up to see what they wanted — just as the warriors were brandishing their tomahawks at Joe.

The Bold decided to wait a while. He was amazed at the sight of Bridger's camp, which included a thousand horses and mules, besides all the people. Perhaps it would be wise to act friendly and use Joe as an interpreter. So the chief ordered his warriors not to harm the captive — yet.

"Tell the white man to come here," said The Bold to Joe Meek.

Joe pretended to do as he was told. But what he really yelled was, "Stay back. Tell Jim Bridger that Joe Meek will be killed if he doesn't come and talk with the chief and get me away."

The guard was back at Bridger's camp in no time, and Jim quickly rode out on a big white horse.

"What tribe is it?" Jim called as he approached.

"Crows," Joe shouted back.

"Tell the head chief to send a subchief to talk to me," Bridger ordered.

The Bold sent a chief named Little Gun out ahead of his own party. Little Gun laid down his weapons, as was the custom when a peaceful talk was to go on. When he met Bridger, he embraced him as another sign of friendship. Then he and Bridger smoked a peace pipe together.

Meanwhile Joe still felt very uneasy. He saw the Crow warriors around him putting on war paint and preparing for battle. He hoped Bridger's men were doing something, too.

They were.

Five Mountain Men sneaked up and took Little Gun prisoner. Joe might be killed any minute for this treachery in the midst of a peace talk. But Jim Bridger's men had moved quickly. When the Crows looked around, they saw a hundred guns aiming straight at them.

"Tell The Bold to exchange you for Little Gun," Bridger shouted.

Joe Meek translated the message. The Bold was furious, but he gave in.

"I cannot afford to lose a chief for one white dog's scalp," he growled.

Joe Meek walked toward Bridger's camp a free man, and Little Gun returned to his people, picking up his weapons as he went.

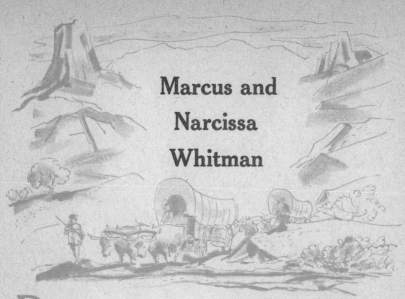

Marcus and Narcissa Whitman

Doctor," said Jim Bridger, "could you do something about this arrowhead in my back? It tickles a little too sharp."

"If you can bear the pain, I'll take it out," Dr. Marcus Whitman answered.

Jim had stood all kinds of hardship, and he figured he could stand this too. No one had heard of anesthetics in those days. And no one on the western side of the Rockies had ever seen a doctor either, at the annual meeting of trappers and traders, until this year, 1835.

Mountain Men and Indians gathered around as Marcus Whitman prepared his sharp knives. It was only his second day at the rendezvous, as the trappers' get-together was called, and he hadn't come to be a doctor — or to trade furs. He was a teacher and a missionary. He had come to talk to Indians about setting up a school and mission. But, if there was medical work to be done, he could do it.

The point of the iron arrowhead was bent and stuck in some cartilage. That was why Jim's own men had not been able to get it out. The doctor had a job cutting it loose. But he worked skillfully, and Jim bore the pain in silence. At last Whitman pulled out the arrowhead.

Here was a man who could work greater wonders than any Indian medicine man. Indians who saw what he did invited Whitman to come and live with them and teach them. This was just what he wanted. And Bridger was so grateful that he acted as guide when the doctor started out to locate a spot for his new mission.

Next year there was an even bigger event at the rendezvous. Marcus Whitman returned, and with him came two figures that made the trappers rub their eyes. Two women — no doubt about it — trotted into camp riding sidesaddle. One was Narcissa Whitman, the wife of Marcus. The other was Eliza Spaulding, the wife of a man who had come to help at the Whitman mission.

No white woman had ever crossed the Rockies before. Indian women swarmed around the two palefaced visitors and kissed them. Mountain Men rushed to shake hands with them. Joe Meek arranged a celebration in honor of these two brave women who had made the long, dangerous trip — and who still had a long way to go before they reached their destination in Oregon.

Marcus Whitman built his mission in Oregon. Then, after six years there, he received a disturbing message.

"The mission committee has decided not to spend any more money on us," Marcus told Narcissa. "I have to go

back East, to Boston. I must persuade the committee to change their minds."

"You can't cross the Rockies in winter," experienced trappers told him.

"But I have to save the mission," Marcus answered. "People from the States are moving into Oregon. Now white children as well as Indian need our school." And he started out.

"Wait till spring," a trader advised him when he reached the Rockies. "You can't cross in winter."

"If you don't travel you can't get there," Whitman stubbornly replied.

Wearing a buffalo-skin overcoat and hood over his buckskin clothes, he headed into the mountains. With him were two companions. They all rode Indian ponies, and mules carried their packs.

Soon the three men were lost in a blizzard. The snow was so deep that the mules and horses could climb only a short distance each day. More blizzards slowed them up.

They ran out of food. Marcus and his friends had to kill their pack animals one by one.

At last the men saw something ahead.

"The pass!" They had reached a high divide in the mountains. From now on they would be going down toward timber. But they could find no game to kill in the deep snow, and they were almost at the end of their strength.

Then suddenly it seemed to Marcus that the air had changed. He couldn't tell at first what the difference was. He took a deep breath. He sniffed.

"Smoke!" he cried. Smoke meant other human beings. Through deep snowdrifts, the three men followed the smell.

The smoke was real. It came from a cabin where some hunters were spending the winter. When Marcus regained his strength they gave him directions, and he struggled on to Taos, far to the south where New Mexico is now. From there, he had a long, cold ride east on the Santa Fe Trail. More than once he nearly froze to death on the treeless plains, but he forced himself to go on.

In the end he reached Boston and saved his mission. Then he returned to Oregon and took many new settlers with him.

"If you don't travel you can't get there," he kept telling them whenever they grew discouraged.

Kit Carson

Seventeen-year-old Kit Carson spent all day, every day, in a saddlemaker's shop. He was what was called an apprentice. This meant that he had to work for almost no money while he was learning his trade — and he couldn't leave his job. He felt like a slave, and he didn't like the saddlemaker.

Kit lived in the little frontier town of Franklin, Missouri. Day after day he repaired saddles or made new ones for men who had wonderful tales to tell about adventures in the Rocky Mountains. And big wagon trains kept going through Franklin on the way to or from the romantic Mexican town of Santa Fe. It was more than Kit could stand to be cooped up at a workbench when there was an exciting world to explore in the West.

"I'm going to run away," Kit decided one day as a wagon train started for Santa Fe. No sooner had he decided, than he acted. That was the way Kit was.

He got a job herding horses for the wagon train. At seventeen Kit couldn't read or write, and he never learned to, but he became one of the most famous men in the West.

Horse Thieves

Kit had a job one winter trapping beavers for a man named Gaunt. A band of friendly Arapahoes was camped nearby. Kit discovered that Gaunt was getting the Arapahoes drunk and buying their buffalo robes for almost nothing. One thing Kit never could stand was a cheat.

"I'm makin' tracks out of here," he said.

Angrily he saddled his horse and rode out of the mountains toward the plains where he had heard William and

Charles Bent were building a huge trading post called Bent's Fort on the Arkansas River.

The Bent brothers knew about Kit Carson, and they hired him at once. Kit's first task was to take a dozen men out and cut logs needed to finish the big fort.

One night in the logging camp he made one of his rare mistakes of carelessness. Instead of tying the horses close to camp, he let them loose to graze on the sparse dry winter grass.

Luckily, two Cheyennes, named Black Whiteman and Little Turtle, dropped in for a visit, and they didn't make the same mistake. They tied their horses near the place where they slept, and the animals were still there in the morning. But Kit's were gone!

Tracks in the snow that had fallen during the night showed that a large party of Crows had sneaked up on foot, captured the horses and ridden them triumphantly away.

"Crows!" Kit exclaimed in surprise. "What are they doing, a thousand miles from home? Come on — we'll git those horses back!"

Immediately he and a dozen men started on foot to follow the Crows. Black Whiteman and Little Turtle went along, too, riding their ponies.

The trail was easy to see in the snow, and by late afternoon Kit knew he had caught up with the horse thieves. A wisp of smoke rose in a willow grove ahead.

"Spread out," Kit ordered the men, "and walk slowly toward the trees. We'll see what we'll see."

The two Cheyennes dropped back out of sight and rode their ponies around to the far side of the grove.

In a moment, Kit knew the Crows had seen his men approaching. A puff of steam went up in the grove where there had been smoke before. That meant the Crows had thrown snow on their small fire to put it out. Night was coming, and firelight would help the white men.

Kit wondered what the Crows planned to do next. Suddenly he found out. Sixty warriors, armed with bows and arrows and tomahawks, leaped yelling out of the grove and charged the thirteen white men.

"Fire!" Kit shouted. The Mountain Men blazed away with their guns.

As suddenly as they had appeared, the Crows slipped back among the trees. They saw no sense in standing out in the open to face men who had guns and who didn't scare easily. The way to fight men on foot was to charge into them on horseback. The Crows ran for their horses.

But the animals had disappeared! While the Crows had been on one side of the grove, preparing to surprise Kit and his men, Black Whiteman and Little Turtle on the other side of the grove had quietly run off all the horses.

It was the Crows' turn now to be afoot, facing men who had horses as well as guns. The warriors fled across the prairie in the growing dusk. Kit and his tired men camped cheerfully for the night — but with a guard over the horses. Kit seldom made the same mistake twice.

Kit Carson Meets Comanches

Comanches were the best horsemen of the Plains. At least, they had the best horses. Young men of the tribe got their mounts by raiding the ranches owned by Mexicans

in Texas and far south of the Rio Grande. No tribe was more bold and fearless — or more fiercely determined to keep its hunting grounds. Comanches wasted no pity on poachers they found in their country.

Kit Carson knew this. But he always went where he pleased and did what he pleased. One day he decided to hunt in Texas. He understood the risks, but he was fearless himself and a superb shot. And he trusted the men who could go with him.

One was Bill Mitchell who had lived as a Comanche for years and who still liked to dress Comanche style — that is, naked except for moccasins and a breechclout. Another was harum-scarum Joe Meek who made up in courage and skill what he lacked in caution. Then there were three Delaware Indians — all good shots and trained from boyhood to fight. The Delaware tribe, not so long before, had been pushed out of New Jersey and Pennsylvania by white men. All across the continent they had fought both white men and other Indians on whose lands they tried to settle.

Kit and these five men jogged along on their tough mules over the treeless prairie, looking for buffalo skins, not scalps, but they felt ready for anything.

"Comanches!" Bill Mitchell shouted one spring morning. He had spotted a scout on a rise of land far ahead.

In no time, two hundred horsemen were charging across the prairie. Their screaming war cry told Kit this was no party coming to welcome the visitors and invite them to make themselves at home in Texas.

"Kill the mules!" Kit ordered. Each man slit the throat

of his animal. Then all together they hauled the carcasses into a circle to use for protection.

The Comanches streamed on toward the six men who now scratched frantically at the earth with their knives to dig a better fortification.

"You three fire first," Kit said to the Delawares. "While you're loading, the rest of us will fire. We don't dare have all our guns empty at once." It took time to ram new powder and lead into the muzzle of a gun after each shot. Kit and his men would be helpless against Comanche arrows and lances unless some of them were always ready to shoot.

On galloped the magnificent Mexican horses. A chief rode out ahead. The three Delawares drew a bead on him. If he fell, it would frighten the Comanches much more than if three other warriors fell.

The Delawares took their time. Only when the chief was almost up to the little fortress did they fire. He rolled off his horse. The rest of the charging warriors swept by on either side, then wheeled and charged back. Kit, Bill, and Joe brought down two of them.

Again the Comanches swept past. This time they paused, but they were too close. The Delawares got another warrior. And still not an arrow had touched Kit and his men.

Evidently the Comanches had decided to use their lances. On they rode, but at the last moment their horses balked! Not one horse would come close enough to the dead mules for a warrior to thrust his lance. The smell of blood frightened the horses off.

As the Comanches drew back out of range, Kit and the

others stood up insolently and jeered. Kit always made it a rule to show that he wasn't afraid.

But the Comanches weren't through by any means. Again and again they charged. Finally their medicine man led an attack. Only when he fell did their confidence waver. They decided to let the hated intruders suffer for a while without water in the hot Texas sun.

From time to time, warriors rode out and circled the little fort that the six men kept digging deeper into the ground. But now the Comanches had grown more cautious. As each warrior circled, he slid over onto the far side of his horse, holding himself on with one arm through a loop of hair in the mane and one heel on the horse's back. From under his animal's neck he shot arrows toward the dead mules.

Kit and his men kept shooting, but they hit only horses now. The Comanches were getting smart. Finally they decided it wasn't worth risking any more horses or men. Away they went!

Kit's party waited to leave until early the next day. Traveling on foot at a steady jog-trot, they headed north out of Comanche country. They had to go eighty miles before they finally reached water, but Kit and his five friends made it.

John C. Fremont

Twelve-year-old Randolph Benton could hardly believe his good luck. Here he stood, this June day in 1842, on the deck of a little steamboat going up the Missouri River. Randolph was the youngest member of an exploring party, on his way to the Rocky Mountains.

He looked with interest at the buckskin-clad men on board. They would be his constant companions for months to come. Now and then his eyes turned to the handsome young Army officer, Lieutenant John C. Fremont who had married his sister and who was in charge of the party.

"Do you know anything about the mountains?" Randolph heard Fremont ask a rather small stranger.

"Reckon I do. Why do you ask?"

"I need a guide to South Pass and beyond," Fremont answered. "The guide I hired has disappeared."

"I can take you to South Pass as easy as a beaver can smell bait."

Randolph followed Fremont around the deck and listened to the inquiries he made about the small stranger, whose name was Kit Carson.

"Know him?" one old fellow said. "Who don't? Kit Carson is the best trapper in the mountains."

It didn't take Fremont long to decide that Kit Carson was the man to guide the expedition. Kit had learned all about the mountains in his trapping days. But the fur trade was now almost a thing of the past. For one thing, the beavers were getting scarce. More important, men's fashions had changed. They no longer wore felt hats made from beaver fur. Kit Carson's trapping days were over, so he was glad for a job as a guide.

For months, Randolph Benton stuck close to the great frontiersman, and he learned how to track men or animals, how to sleep in the open, how to hunt buffalo — how to live among the Indians of the Wild West.

Everything about the trip was exciting — even the reason for it. Randolph knew that his father, the famous Senator Benton in Washington, had persuaded the Army to send Fremont to the West. He knew Papa was interested in finding out all he could about the West, so that settlers could go there to live. Senator Benton wanted these settlers to be men who worked their own farms, not slaveholders.

Right now Texas was asking to join the Union — with slavery allowed. Many people didn't want to let Texas into the Union until they could balance it with a no-slave state — or many no-slave states — in the West. So this expedition was part of a big plan to have the West settled by men who, like Senator Benton, didn't want slavery to spread.

Fremont was just the man to find out about this vast new country. He loved the wilderness, and when this first expedition was over, he took Kit Carson along on more exploring trips to the remotest parts of the continent — through great areas that even Kit had never visited.

Doing the Impossible

It was February, and the high Sierra Nevada Mountains stood between Fremont and California, the territory he was determined to explore.

"I'm sure we can get across," he said to Kit Carson, and he told his men to make snowshoes and sleds.

Wearing snowshoes, he and Kit scouted ahead. They zigzagged uphill for ten miles over snow that was anywhere from five to twenty feet deep. At the top of a divide, a great view to the west opened out in front of the weary pair.

"See that little mountain?" Kit pointed. "I remember it. Now I know exactly where we are." He hadn't seen the mountain for fifteen years, but he had an amazing memory. "We can make it. Look below. Grass for the horses."

Then a terrific struggle began. Men used huge blocks of wood on long handles to pound down the snow, beating a path for the horses. It was slow, exhausting work.

The weather grew colder. More snow fell. Food supplies ran out. Fremont's men began to kill their horses. For ten days they fought their way, just to cover the terrible ten miles up to the divide.

At last the weary party left the arctic weather of the mountains and came out into what Fremont called "the Perpetual Spring" of the Sacramento Valley. There he and his ragged men and starved animals rested and regained their strength.

There was one man who especially found the land to his liking. This was Jacob Dobson, a free Negro who had come with Fremont on the long hard trip.

As for Fremont, his enthusiasm grew by the minute. Here was indeed a land where free Americans could prosper.

Brigham Young

Brigham Young loved to walk about the town of Nauvoo, Illinois, with its comfortable houses of brick and stone and its huge Mormon church that the people were building. Young was himself a leader in the church, and he hoped that its members would be allowed to live here in their town undisturbed. But in the autumn of 1845 he grew sad, then angry, because of the terrible reports he heard. Groups of armed men kept attacking his friends who had built Nauvoo and made it into the biggest town west of Pittsburgh.

These lawless gangs disagreed with the Mormon religion, and they didn't believe in freedom of worship. In addition, they wanted to drive the prosperous Mormons away so they could get their farms.

"My house and barn were burned today!" one man told Young.

"My cattle were killed!"

"My husband was shot!"

Brigham Young asked for protection from the officials of Illinois. No help came.

"We have to move in order to save our lives," he said at last. "I have read Colonel Fremont's report of his journey beyond the Rockies. Somewhere out there we will find the right place. We must settle where nobody else lives. We must find a new home where nobody will attack us."

By now winter had come, and the Mississippi River was filled with ice. Young knew this was a bad time to lead twelve thousand people into the wilderness. Still, there was

nothing else he could do. It would be a harder job than any pioneer had ever tried before. Where could all his people get food as they traveled? Where could thousands of horses and mules and oxen and milk cows find enough grass to eat?

"Somehow we will manage," he said grimly. "We have to — if we want to live."

Little homemade boats carried people, horses, cattle, wagons across the big river. Bitter cold filled the tents that the Mormon people had to camp in, only seven miles from their warm homes. Many of them had no food at all for themselves or their animals; the armed mobs had destroyed their crops.

"We must share what we have," Young said.

The people kept on sharing everything as the great wagon train started west in the spring. The prairie was so muddy, and the animals were so weak from hunger, that the caravan could travel only about two and a half miles a day. Brigham Young saw that he and his followers would die of starvation if they tried to push right on to the Rockies.

"There is only one thing to do," he announced. "We must stop and grow some food."

When they reached the Missouri River, the wagons stopped. People began to build log cabins and to plant crops. Here they would spend the winter, getting ready for the long trip across the plains.

Not everybody agreed with all of Brigham Young's decisions, but they had to admit he was a brave and sensible man. He had good ideas about little things as well as big ones, and that made him a remarkable leader indeed.

First of all, he kept every man, woman, and child busy. Some of them made equipment and clothes for the journey that was still ahead of them. Others made milking stools and washboards and baskets that they could trade for food when they went past cabins along the way.

But it wasn't enough for twelve thousand people just to be busy. Brigham Young knew they had to be cheerful, too. Luckily, all the members of a brass band had joined the Mormon church, which its members called the Church of Jesus Christ of the Latter-day Saints. So Young arranged for band concerts at night. He organized dances and community sings. In spite of sickness and misery, the huge camp of log cabins and sod huts buzzed with activity. Everything went according to plans that Young worked out.

"Where are we going to settle?" the others kept asking Brigham Young.

Young wouldn't answer the question, but he did ask

questions of his own when he pushed on with an advance party and began to meet Mountain Men.

"What about the country around the Salt Lake?" Young said to an old trapper who was called Peg Leg Smith.

"Nothing grows there, and there's no game," Peg Leg answered.

Still Young kept questioning.

"The Salt Lake country ain't fit to live in," Jim Bridger said.

Young listened to these reports, and instead of being dismayed he was delighted. But he was careful not to show it. He felt sure that Bridger and Peg Leg Smith didn't know what they were talking about. The soil was undoubtedly good for farming,

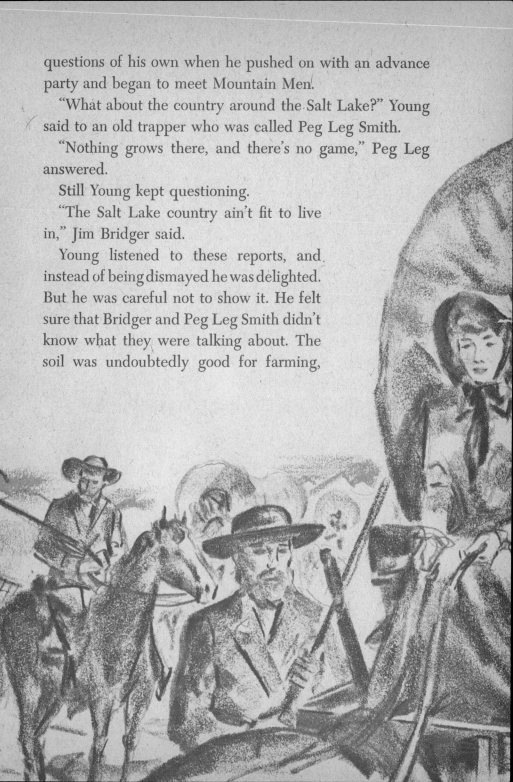

because Fremont had said so. And if these Mountain Men frightened others away from the Salt Lake, that was fine. This meant the Mormons would have the place to themselves. There would be no neighbors to bother them — which was exactly what they wanted most.

So Young turned his wagons toward the great unsettled land of Utah, which belonged to Mexico at that time. There the Mormons would make their new home.

"This is the right place," Brigham Young said when he first looked out from a hilltop at the tremendous view of the Salt Lake Valley.

After his party reached the bottom of the mountain, they weren't so sure. The earth was dry. At first glance the soil looked black. And then they realized that it was simply alive with fat, black crickets! Grimly Young remembered Fremont's story that the Indians — and sometimes also the Mountain Men — got so hungry in this country that they ate roasted crickets.

Nevertheless Brigham Young and his farmer-pioneers put their seeds into the ground near the Great Salt Lake, and with water from the mountain streams they irrigated the dry land.

Before long they had turned the desert into a garden.

Buffalo Bill

Ten-year-old William Cody lived near the Kickapoo Indian Reservation in Kansas, where his father ran a store. He played with the Indian boys, spoke their language, rode a horse as well as any of them, and was already a good shot with a rifle. It was exciting to live on the frontier. What's more, a war was going on between two groups of Kansas settlers in the year 1856. Some settlers were for slavery in Kansas; some were against. Billy Cody's father was against.

One day Billy's father climbed up on a drygoods box amidst a crowd of people and said:

"I pledge you my word I shall lay down my life if need

be to keep the curse of slavery from growing up on Kansas soil."

A moment later Billy saw a bowie knife in the hand of a man who favored slavery. The man jumped onto the box, plunged the knife into Billy's father, and killed him.

At the age of eleven, Billy had to go to work to support his family. By the time he was fourteen he had a man's job, earning a man's wages. He carried the mail on the new Pony Express.

Billy was a superb rider, and he gained fame as the youngest of the many young men who galloped long distances, changing horses frequently, as they rushed the mail across the plains and mountains to and from California.

Later, young William got a job killing buffalo to feed the men who were building railroads across the continent. He killed 69 buffalo in one day and 4,862 in one season. That's why people nicknamed him Buffalo Bill.

Wild Bill
Hickok

When Buffalo Bill Cody was eleven years old, he went to work on a train of freight wagons. One day, when they stopped for a rest, some of the freight drivers started to rough him up.

A tall young man, who lay in the shade, under one of the wagons, saw what was going on, and he didn't like it.

"What are you doing to that boy?" he demanded, crawling out from under the wagon.

"Mind your own business," said a driver.

If there was one thing the young man couldn't stand it was a bully who tried to push other people around.

"Want to fight?" he said. "Then you can tackle me — and let the kid alone."

The drivers decided to let them both alone. Something about the determined air of the big twenty-year-old told them they'd better find another way to amuse themselves.

James Butler Hickok was the youth's name, but everybody called him "Wild Bill." How he got the nickname was a mystery, for he certainly wasn't wild. In fact, he stood out among the boisterous frontiersmen because he was so quiet and gentlemanly. But the name stuck.

When the Civil War came along, John C. Fremont got in touch with Wild Bill. Fremont was a general in the Union Army now, and he knew a good frontier scout when he saw one. He put Wild Bill in charge of supply wagons in Missouri and Kansas. From there Bill moved on and became a spy behind Confederate lines.

After the war, he drifted from one wild frontier town to another. Time and again he got into gun fights with bullies on the rampage. Sometimes he was the town marshal when the shooting started. Sometimes he was just an ordinary citizen who wouldn't be "put upon"— which was his way of saying he wouldn't be pushed around. Either way, Wild Bill never killed for the sake of killing.

The days of gun-toting have long since passed. So have the stubborn, ingenious pioneers who led the way to a land so rich that many millions of people can live on it. But the pioneer spirit is not dead. There are no more Wild West frontiers for daring men to explore. The frontiersmen of today are busy in new places. They explore the icy wastes of Antarctica, the depths of the world's vast oceans, and the endless distances of outer space.